The Business of Audio Engineering

By Dave Hampton

TEACHER'S GUIDE

Thank you for adopting this book into your Music Business course curriculum. Please use this guide to assist you in preparing your lectures and course work. This material is written so that you can simultaneously educate and evaluate each student's progress. The main goal of this course is to give students an interactive way to recognize their value and to be able to effectively create and maintain business relationships. The questions have been formed so that you can see on an individual level how the students process the information from the lessons and how they will potentially make decisions in the professional world.

Chapter 1: Education and Training
Chapter 2: Building Confidence

Questions and topics for discussion:

∞ Discuss how each student got interested in their career.

∞ What do they want to get out of their education?

∞ Give examples of what is meant by the expression, "Getting your foot in the door."

∞ What does the phrase, "little money is money too" mean?

∞ Discuss each student having a personal vision for his or her career.

Chapter 3: Professionalism
Chapter 4: Follow your Instinct

Questions and topics for discussion:

∞ Discus students' impression of the story, Less Than Half.

∞ List some of the observations made about the characters in the story.

∞ Hampton writes, "Your dollars are directly related to your productivity." What does he mean?

∞ Why is it important to know which role you play on a project?

∞ Name some of the tips for new engineers to standout (highlighted in dark print: 11 total).

∞ Why is it important to understand the responsibilities that go with the pay grade?

∞ Explain what the author meant when he wrote, "The deal you cut is the deal you cut."

∞ Discuss the importance of the concept of putting "real business" on paper.

∞ Discuss the second paragraph on page 34. Does the Yin/Yang principle describe some kind of justification for doing wrong?

∞ Have each student explain how they have learned to recognize "good and bad' behavior patterns in business…and in life.

∞ How important are instincts?

∞ Discuss some of the students' first thoughts and instincts in different situations.

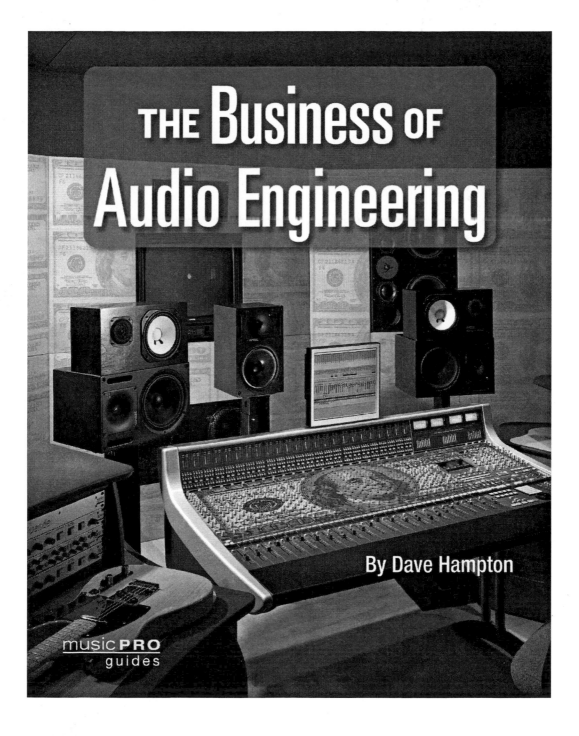

THE Business OF Audio Engineering

By Dave Hampton

musicPRO guides

TEACHER'S GUIDE

Instinct Exercise:

- ∞ Have the students do a quick stem mix of recorded material using only their instincts as engineers to mix and give the tracks a direction. (This exercise is relevant because engineers must use their instinct for both the music and life/business decisions.)

- ∞ Give the students these scenarios where they must choose their action step based on instincts:
    - o **Scenario 1:** They have an opportunity for a post production gig right out of school, but the project calls for an audio edit and soundtrack for a porno movie. Their religious beliefs have them wondering if this is the gig for them. The money is good for someone right out of school. What do they do?
    - o **Scenario 2:** A classmate has a recording deal and wants someone in the studio that they trust to engineer the record. The money is good and the studio is famous. They have no experience in a real session as the lead engineer- just the trust of their classmate. Do they take the job?
    - o **Scenario 3:** They got a job engineering for the latest hot young artist. The artist likes to get high when they record. Do you join in?

Note: The correct response in the first two cases is to do what is comfortable. In the second scenario the best response is to meet with the schoolmate and let them know you are interested in doing the gig but you must be honest about your lack of experience. While you understand the comfort level that was shared at school, you would feel better working with them knowing that you are green. Taken from real life, the third scenario could possibly get your teeth knocked out of your head. This actually happened to an engineer who missed a punch-in on a vocal and got punched out because he was more worried about fitting in and getting high than paying attention.

Chapter 5: Reputations
Chapter 6: Commitment vs. Involvement

Questions and topics for discussion:

- ∞ Have each student answer why their own reputation is important to them.

- ∞ Discuss the author's reference to the "power of a handshake."

∞ Have the students give examples of the importance of a good reputation and how it applies to our business.

∞ Discuss the students' feelings about the author saying, "We are at a time in history when even well-educated people have no guarantee of making it."

Reputation Exercise:

∞ Propose a new gig opportunity to your students. Tell them each person is in charge of hiring their own crew.
∞ Have them write down the names of two other students that they want to work with on paper. Then have them turn in the papers to you.

As you unfold the names, you will find that 2-3 students' names always come up.

Conclusion: The students whose names repeatedly come up are the ones who have a good reputation. They have already begun to brand themselves.

∞ Have the students read and discuss the Radio Ranch Story.

∞ Have the students describe the difference between commitment and involvement in their own words.

Important point to discuss: Never waste everyone's time by discussing what is not possible!

∞ Discuss these lessons from the story:

   1. Listen to your client
   2. Knowledge is power
   3. Pick your battles
   4. Arrogance gets no check

Chapter 7: Picking Clients
Chapter 8: How Do I Really Get A Job?

Questions and topics for discussion:

∞   Give examples of, "Some kinds of money costs too much to make."

∞   What are "referrals"?

∞   Ask the students for their ideas on how to get clients and generate work.

∞   Ask students how they would have handled the audio book editing story.

∞   In the first paragraph of page 76, the author doesn't just turn down a gig but he refers an engineer he feels is better suited for the client's situation. Why would he do this?

∞   What is the difference between working with someone vs. telling someone what to do?

∞   What is meant by the statement, "It's a business of friends"?

∞   Have students use the website resources to give examples of how information can be used to find jobs. Research websites where they can post their skills and announce that they are ready to be hired, like

Chapter 9: Knowing Your Value
Chapter 10: Wages & Job Opportunities

Questions and topics for discussion:

∞   What do the terms commitment and responsibility mean to each student?

∞   Discuss what the students understand the term "fair wage" to mean.

∞ Have students give examples of "creative deals" (internship & employment).

∞ Have each student list all the skills and talents that they have. Please include any second languages, special certifications, and additional education.

∞ Explain why the author wrote, "Give my name to ten people."

∞ Why is the "Put It on Paper" principal so important?

Chapter 10 uses comparative analysis. Have the students use the tables to figure out what skills they have to charge for services.

∞ Why would the author use these three jobs described on pages 111 & 112?

∞ Have each student explain the difference between a skill and a tactic.

∞ Discuss some ways in which each student can create their own door into the business.

∞ The author warns about "unfulfilled desires". Why?

Chapter 11: Independent Contracting vs. Corporate America

Questions and topics for discussion:

Read the Q &A and discuss the answers and examine any reoccurring themes.

Chapter 12: Legally Forming Your Company

Questions and topics for discussion:

Read this section and discuss the options for some of your students. Incorporation is not for everyone. Help your students find their own starting point.

Chapter 13: Setting Up Long Money Situations

Questions and topics for discussion:

Using the example in the story below, have the students lay out a plan that shows how they will create cash flow with their new skills.

Hustlenomics 101

Here are some notes on how to create a financial start when you leave school. Many students will find themselves out of school waiting for their big break while they hopefully find some studio situations to intern at. The following information is what I gave to my son upon his graduation from audio school.

He and I were discussing what his next move was. He told me, "Dad I need to get my paper (money) straight!" I asked him what his plan was. He proceeded to let me know that he was interning (working for free) at a local voice over studio three days a week. In addition he had a part time job at a law office making $10.00/hr.

I quickly asked him what his monthly expenses were. He roughly gave me the figures and with rent (he has a roommate) and utilities in LA, the expenses for this 22 year old male fresh out of audio school came to about $1,750.00.

In addition, I asked him what his rate for doing audio work in his home studio. He told me he was charging $25.00/hr. Here is a formula that I put into place based on his situation:

Income from recording:

Studio engineering for a minimum of 3hrs/day, 5 days/week= **15 hours**

15 hours @ $25.00/hr. = **$375.00**

$375.00 x 4 weeks/month = **$1,500.00/ month**

Income from legal job:

Legal office work for 8hrs/day, 3 days/week= **24 hours**

24 hours @ $10.00/hr. = **$240.00**

$240.00 x 4 weeks/month = **$960.00**

Between the consistent job and the independent job doing audio, he can easily generate **$2,460.00.** If we subtract the monthly expenses of $1,750.00 it leaves **$710.00** for savings. By saving a minimum of $250.00/month for one year you actually create a savings of $3,000.00 plus interest. Now this is just a quick start scenario but just imagine how much more money could be made by doing the following:

- ∞ **Decrease the number of hours on the legal job.**
- ∞ **Increase the number of independent hours.**
- ∞ **Cut down on expenses.**
- ∞ **Create independent job stability by filling your calendar with paid audio work. This means engineering and other related work that gets you your $25.00/hr (or more).**
- ∞ **Wean yourself off of the $10.00/hr gig and invest in yourself and your independence.**

Here is something to think about. Years ago the main job (the 9-5) was the thing that had stability. Now in today's economy the independent "hustle" job is often the stronger performer. With the national average for a work week being 40+ hours, as a young engineer starting out, would you rather work 15 hours and make $375.00 or work 24 hours to make $240.00?

Chapter 14: Visualization

Questions and topics for discussion:

- ∞ Have each student comment on what visualization means to them.

- ∞ Consider giving them extra credit for taking the time to write to the author with their thoughts and reflections on the material in this book.

- ∞ Review the websites and additional information in the rear of the book. Use them to enhance your approach to preparing your class materials.